A FREE THINKER

ON GOD AND RELIGION

A FREE THINKER

ON GOD AND RELIGION

BRIG DARSHAN KHULLAR

Vij Books India Pvt Ltd

New Delhi (India)

First Published in India in 2021

Published by

Vij Books India Pvt Ltd
(Publishers, Distributors & Importers)
2/19, Ansari Road
Delhi – 110 002
Phones: 91-11-43596460, 91-11-47340674
Mob: 98110 94883
e-mail: contact@vijpublishing.com
web : www.vijbooks.in

In loving memory of my son Ajay.

CONTENTS

INTRODUCTION

This is not a religious book, but it is a book about God and religion. I do not claim to be a great scholar in the realm of metaphysics, but I have been fascinated by the role of religion in the lives of humans. I have no intention of hurting the religious sentiments of any person or community, but I have my doubts and there are many thoughts which just will not go away, which I would like to share with the like-minded readers. I am not an atheist. An atheist, I believe, apart from being a rationalist must be mentally strong with self-belief and he must be a highly detached person emotionally. Also, most rationalists tend to be fanatics in their own ways. I consider myself to be a free thinker.

I believe there is a supreme force that defies description. There is enough rational and scientific evidence and data that should leave one with no doubt that the universe had a beginning which could have been created by only some enormously intelligent super-entity. Everything in this world and indeed the universe is indicative of a grand design and purpose. You may ask what was there before the beginning and what lies beyond the universe. It is a riddle that the scientists will solve at some stage. I find the idea of there being a personal God perplexing and even problematic.

The earth is a mere spec in the universe and we humans are too insignificant in the universal scheme of things and yet have giant-sized egos. From childhood, through knowledge gained by word of mouth, via religious books, mythologies and kindred folklore celebrating our God [gods] and secular education, we learn geography and history and, in the process, acquire a vicarious sense of participation and a feeling as if we have always been there.   We cannot reconcile to our brief stay in this world which incidentally is among the longest among most animal species and therefore have invented for ourselves the concept of before and after life because at the heart of the matter is the quest of immortality to get over the fear of death and mortality. But this is fallacious because if we genuinely and wholeheartedly believed in an afterlife, we should not be fearing death any longer.

We are a product of nature. Nature as we know it is water, earth, fire, atmosphere, metal, stone, vegetable, and animal kingdoms and more. All laws of nature are profoundly scientific though our knowledge as it presently exists is mere scratching of the surface. Do we know whether the nature has a mind that directs all its actions? Humans we know have an intelligence, but we cannot see it. Similarly, Nature seems to be possessed of some terrible invisible power or supreme intelligence, the eternal being which directs all its operations? How can man profess to know what even Nature cannot know?

In the nature there is interplay of science and an infinity of art. All that we see around us has a scientific basis, but there is great art in every manifestation of nature. Those vast oceans and their satellite seas, awesome mountains, highlands, forests, valleys, vast plains, steppes, and deserts are all works of great art. Those high snow clad mountains that crown the earth are immense reservoirs of fresh water and because of them there are unceasing fountains, brooks, subsoil water, lakes, and rivers without which the animal species and vegetable species would perish. Reflect for a moment on the phenomenon of rain and snowfall that makes all this possible. Imagine the mindboggling waterworks and infrastructure that would be required to distill the sea water and then pump all this from the seas and oceans to all corners of the globe? It is beyond human capacity and yet nature has done it so magnificently. Ever so many million years there is an ice age for the nature to keep the cycle going. The way all living species have been made is itself a miracle. Consider for once the creation of an insect, leave alone the higher species, or of an abundance of flora, even an ear of corn, of variety of minerals [gold, iron, copper and so on], everything is a marvel of science and art created by some superlatively potent and ingenious mighty being, who hides himself while making nature appear.

It is our destiny that we get to nourish ourselves ever so briefly, drinking a few drops of its milk and then dying without knowing the mother that has nursed us. Will we ever know why the universe and everything in it exists, this multitude of existences made only for continuous dissolution, this host of animals to be born only to devour and to be devoured, this host of sentient beings created to endure so much pleasure, pain, and suffering? Would not nothingness be better?

What I have reproduced in the four paragraphs above are the thoughts of Voltaire, one of the world's greatest thinkers of all times, so apt, that I thought I should share for the reader's benefit.

THE IDEA OF GOD

The belief in God is as old as human race itself, though the concept has varied widely across the centuries with emergence of often conflicting religions. It is the primeval fear factor, especially the fear of the unknown which has made God/gods and in the process religions all pervasive and with that have followed all kinds of beliefs and even superstitions. There is a God nucleus in our brains. Humans are wired for religious belief. It is as though God wants us to keep singing his praise and praying to him. Surely God cannot be so egoistic and insecure. A plausible explanation is that it is some quirk in the revolutionary process that is the cause of it all.

People may worship one God or many gods, but they do not necessarily worship the same God/gods because their conceptions of what and whom they worship are seldom the same. In fact, we all feel that ours is the right path at the exclusion of others. Some believe in rebirth, reincarnation, and karma while others believe that you live once and go to heaven or hell or stay in limbo. There are a thousand vulnerabilities and insecurities that we humans suffer from; it is only belief in a personal God that can sustain us.

On the other hand, there have been rationalist or materialistic philosophies like Epicureanism in Greece and the Carvaka school of thought among the Hindus, and even Buddhism which have questioned the existence of God. But serious questioning seems to have begun only during the period of enlightenment 17th century onwards in Europe.

Baruch Spinoza (1632-1677), a Dutch philosopher regarded God as the Principal Law of nature, the sum of eternal laws. Immanuel Kant (1724-1804), a German considered to be one of the most eminent thinkers in the fields of epistemology and metaphysics declared that only way to God was through practical reason. Voltaire (1694-1778), the famous French historian and philosopher, known for his wit and criticism of Christianity sought a new religion based on reason, justice, and tolerance.

They have been followed by great thinkers and rationalists who have mocked God and religion. To them God is simply a man made phenomenon. Schopenhauer (1788-1860) rejected the western idea of God. Darwin (1809-1882) demolished the book of Genesis. Karl Marx (1818-1883) called religion the opiate of the masses. Nietzsche (1844-1900) pronounced God was dead' Freud (1856-1939) analyzed that the idea of God sprang from an infantile yearning for a protective father figure. Bertrand Russel (1872-1970) called out against the excesses of metaphysics. There have been modern day nay Sayers, outspoken assassins of God like Sam Harris, Daniel Dennett, Christopher Hitchens, and Richard Hawkins who seem to have made a small dent in a section of the liberal society mostly in the West. The number of atheists as per a BBC report has risen in Europe in the last two decades from 3 to 13 percent.

On the other hand, there has been for a variety of reasons a massive religious resurgence across the world, especially among the Muslims, Hindus and even Christians to some extent. Atheism therefore cannot be a substitute for billions of common men (not yet anyway) who want to believe that they have souls and hope to make it to the heaven as defined in their respective faiths where they will get to meet their near and dear ones and be reborn based on their Karma? Science or atheism have so far failed to demolish this belief. Here one should not include the communists because they themselves are victims of an ideology and indoctrination and with their closed minds are incapable of thinking independently. Amongst the Hindus there has always been a presence of atheists and rationalists who like to target the various superstitions, evils, and retrograde practices.

The situation can also change rapidly. The nearly three century long competition between science and religion that has waxed and waned is likely to sharpen considerably with the full fruition of artificial intelligence. It will be a revolutionary event that is bound to cause a major upheaval, its consequences difficult to foretell.

It may presently appear implausible, but it is quite possible that Science may eventually satisfy man's spiritual needs. Will the exploration of the Cosmos lead to spiritual fulfilment? Will we come to a stage when science and religion will merge/ come to coexist? Albert

Einstein had famously remarked "Science without religion is lame and religion without science is blind".

Fact is over the centuries Science has demolished many old myths and beliefs, like for instance it is no longer necessary to invoke the religious texts to explain various natural phenomenon; the axis and orbit of the earth, the magnetic system [North and South poles], the earth's rotation on its axis and revolutions around the Sun resulting in day and night and the seasons. Man has reached the moon and will soon make it to the Mars. Science will continue to expose the religions and the so-called revelations and myths for what they are. May be science will bring about the true realization about the supreme force that controls the cosmos and in the process there will emerge a true religion based on scientific knowledge and spiritualism.

The universe is unfathomable and infinite. It is assumed to be 13.8 billion years old and the earth some 4.5 billion years. A human being has a life span of maximum around 100 years, wherein he experiences childhood, youth, middle and finally old age. A stage comes when one is simply passing time awaiting death. A hundred years appear exceptionally long, it takes great effort to keep going. Imagine a supreme being or force who has been there from the very beginning, un-ageing, eternal, renewing himself endlessly. Evolution is not, therefore, necessarily incompatible with faith. It is a phenomenon that the Supreme Being that we call God has meticulously set-in motion. When we consider the time and space that spans millions and billions of years the extremely slow evolutionary process makes great sense. The Supreme Being is obviously in no hurry and has programmed it all with a cosmic computer that defies definition. Even the process of so-called natural selection has been immaculately designed by God. When the supreme being created the herbivorous animals, he also created the carnivorous species and not without logic. To imagine that the reptiles or whatever developed wings on their own is ridiculous. The vast variety of wilderness, flora, and fauna, the colourful birds and flowers and the scenic beauty are the Divine's gifts to embellish the life on earth. Of course, the opposite is also true and there is ample ugliness, malignancies, sickness, hazards, and abysses and so on. It can be said with fair certainty that the supreme being created man to take over the earth and made available resources, raw material and minerals and laws of nature which he continues to discover and carry out amazing inventions with much effort and scientific endeavor.

As per the law of nature all species have leaders. Among the humans, the countries, states, towns, and villages are run by governments which in turn have various ministries, departments, and bureaucracies etc. Even in the so-called monotheistic religions their founders had their followers and companions to whom they delegated various responsibilities. Consider then the affairs of the universe, God too could have his ministers looking after various portfolios. So, polytheism does make sense. But what does God look like? He is said to be ageless and formless. But that is simply an explanation of convenience. The Hindu gods and goddesses are shown mostly middle aged and have sons, grandsons, daughters, and granddaughters. But there seems to be a status quo ante – no further generations?

There were the Greek and the Egyptian gods of pharaohs' days. They seem to have disappeared once these people converted to Christianity and Islam. Where have these gods gone? Did they ever exist?

HEAVEN AND HELL

Suffering and evil. Why does God who is said to be ever merciful and omnipresent allow these to exist and even proliferate. Evil flourishes and there is great injustice. Often the good suffer and often the wicked prosper. To counter this there is the "Free Will" argument of the theists who believe that God invested humans with free will and cognition, where they have the options to choose voluntarily between good and bad decisions and act accordingly. In Hinduism, Buddhism and Sikhism there is the belief in good and bad karma. It is all very convoluted. Would it not be better if the reward and punishment were to be spontaneous or at least in the same life? Karma makes for fatalistic thinking. Tongue in cheek, Bertrand Russcl had said "It is very plausible that as a matter of fact this world as we know was made by the Devil at a time when God was not looking".

How can one explain away calamities inflicted by humans on humans like shoot outs, terror attacks, road accidents to a war which kills and maims in thousands? Why should the free will of one person be the cause of death and suffering of innumerable innocent persons?

The truth more likely is that none of these suppositions are valid. Answer may lie in the metaphysical laws where the good and evil occur with some definite purpose and unexplainable randomness. It is as though nature has created the opposites to balance the life on this earth and does not differentiate between good and evil who must constantly keep fighting each other in a seesaw battle of sorts.

Evil, violence, disasters, diseases, pestilence, wars and all other negative attributes and manifestations of suffering proliferate in abundance in this world. Violence is inherent in nature. It is in our genes. Our ancestors killed to thrive and survive. We are the only species that kill for pleasure and take great joy in killing fellow beings. Wars are considered righteous and gateways to heaven for the fallen martyrs. Whose side is God on?

It has been said that the world is all Maya- an illusion. It is like a huge stage where we all play our assigned roles of heroes, villains, and extras, perform, procreate, and move on. Being good and bad is not up to us. It is genetics at play. It is all a matter of individual and collective conscience. A psychopath displays no regrets. It is how nature has made him. Men's' views of right and wrong have kept on varying from generation to generation. Evolutionary scientists have suggested that the driving force in evolution is the survival and propagation of genes that make the animal species commit acts of goodness and is also the cause of their selfless behaviour. Every community has a near equal share of good and bad people; the good samaritans, the kind and the compassionate as also the cruel, murderers and cheats and deceivers and so on and religions are the convenient alibis in the process. It is generally the aggressive minority that drives any society.

There is abundance of goodness and beauty, both natural and manmade, leaving little doubt that heaven is here itself on this earth.

The natural beauty abounds amidst mountains, valleys, forests, lakes, flora, and fauna – the wildlife. Man, himself has created ample beauty in the form of beautiful cities, monuments, parks, music, and arts, and wherever there is justice, love, camaraderie, compassion, self- sacrifice and peace, there is heaven. We experience heaven even in domestic bliss more often among the poor. Sex can be heavenly where there is true love.

But hell is also here on this earth through natural and manmade disasters and calamities – through cruelty, hatred, evil, poverty, disease, malevolent forces, and persons, in accidents and tragedies.

For those who think otherwise may be asked this simple question. Where exactly are the Heaven and Hell located? Surely with the astounding strides in space research and astronomy we ought to have some idea about their location or existence. One thing is for certain these are not part of our planetary system and to reach the nearest star would hypothetically take a few million years in a spacecraft and yet in the primitive times space travel was apparently a simple expedient when one could make it to the heavens on horseback and gods and angels soft landed on the earth's surface periodically to confabulate with the chosen ones. Should we be surprised that with the coming of science and its stupendous advances these celestial phenomena no longer occur.

The end of humanity on earth is inevitable at some point of time. There are enough number of manmade and natural disasters like nuclear war, global warming and large-scale pandemic that can make it happen. That these are to a large extent avoidable with human endeavour and understanding should give us hope. But what about the cosmic disasters that lurk in space like asteroid impact, supernova explosions and so on that could simply wipe out life on earth. When it must happen, it will just happen, and it won't be for the first or the last time This is something we cannot change. What we can do is to make the most of our time on Earth. To be fearful will not do. Space should be our inspiration as it offers immense possibilities and the ultimate meaning.

SOUL

Whatever the soul is, science so far has failed to prove or disprove its existence. Some believers have likened it to the wind which moves unseen but with unmistakable effects. Plato had called it the essence of a living thing. Aquinas said that the soul is not made of matter. It is unsubstantial, invisible, and therefore impervious to injury by physical forces. Bhagavat Gita which was written much earlier has described the soul in similar words; It is unborn, eternal, permanent and primeval. It does not die with the body. Just as a person casts off worn-out garments and puts on others that are new, even so does the embodied soul take on others that are new. It is uncleavable, it cannot be burnt, wetted nor dried. It is eternal, all pervading, unchanging, unmanifested and unthinkable.

But what about the functioning of the human brain. Can we ignore its cognitive manifestations? Is there a relationship between the brain and the soul? To quote George Paxinos "The brain is where thinking takes place, love and hatred reside, sensations become perceptions, personality is formed, memories and beliefs are held, and where decisions are made and as D K Johnson has said; there is nothing left for the soul to do". Much before that Hippocrates [460-377 BC] had said "Men ought to know that from nothing else, but the brain comes joys, delights, laughter, sports, sorrows, griefs, sorrows, griefs and lamentations. It is in the brain that we acquire wisdom and knowledge, and see and hear, and know what is foul and what is fair; what is bad, what is good, what is sweet and what is unsavoury".

We all know that accidents, dementia, Alzheimer, and congenital malformations damage the mind. A head injury can make one lose one's memories for good or for several years. What happens to the soul when all this happens, if indeed the soul is formless and separate from the physical being all this should not happen. We also know that deficiency or excess of certain elements like dopamine, noradrenaline and serotonin causes chemical imbalance in the brain and is causally linked to mental illness like depression, schizophrenia, bipolar disorder, paranoia, and psychosis? An attack of encephalitis lethargica can make a virtuous man to become vicious and a clever child can be turned into an idiot by lack of iodine. On the other hand, there are drugs and medicines that help to cure and alleviate these maladies. How then can we say that the brain and soul are separate entities. Possibility therefore that the mind survives when a person becomes brain dead is extremely remote in fact zero.

In good old days, a person undergoing psychotic episodes was considered either possessed by the Devil or other evil spirits and there were also those who were considered as messengers of God and saintly beings, and some went on to form new religions and cults.

Is soul the subconscious or super conscious? But now that the mankind has made unbelievable progress in the field of artificial intelligence and may in the foreseeable future be able to replicate the human brain or upload it on to a robot or computer, we may well discover that the soul is simply a phenomenon of the brain activated by an electric impulse generated by the static electricity present in our physical bodies. And just as the computer shuts down when its battery is removed, similarly when a man dies and with it the static electricity and brain cells, his brain too dies and with that dies the so-called soul unlike in case of a computer where the stored data and hardware can be activated and reactivated as required. May be near death phenomenon experienced by some persons when they usually have suffered cardiac arrest and there is no pulse, but the individual's brain is alive, can be explained by the fact that the brain continuing to retain its cognitive faculty begins to go through a dream sequence depicting an afterlife propelled by the subconscious and they recall all this after they have been revived. One can therefore say that soul is nothing but human intelligence with its many complexities. One wonders what will happen when like thc heart/kidney/ lung transplant our surgeons are able to carry out a brain transplant. Will the recipient lose his original memory or rather the very identity of his original self? Who will he be, person A (the recipient) or person B [the donor} now inhabiting a different body or a hybrid? We will only know when it happens, but the eventuality holds great significance as far as metaphysics or moral science are concerned. Cloning one reckons has similar ramifications.

Notwithstanding the above let us for a moment assume that soul does indeed exist, a kind of hologram that rises from human body and thereafter reaches heaven or hell, certain questions need to be tackled. To feel pain or pleasure including the sexual one with which at least one of the religions is particularly obsessed with, you need flesh and bones, sense and other organs that are part of our living body and so how then does a formless entity get to experience all this in the afterlife. If it is all virtual, then does it amount to anything?

While it is residing inside the body, the soul is quite helpless if you consider the limitations of human capacity and yet we give it supernatural power when it leaves the body unless some spiritual power takes charge of it.

Belief in before and after life, is all based on what religion that you are born into or the one you follow but nobody has ever come back in person to tell you about it.

There are cases reported about people (mostly children) remembering their previous lives, usually in cases where the person concerned died an unnatural death, mostly was murdered. How authentic are such stories? Could there be a scientific explanation?

Is it fair to assume that the brain is a computer cum radio cum transmitter? If so, it must be functioning at a certain frequency and occasionally the message gets transmitted and lodged in a child that is yet in the womb.

At some stage, most of us do experience shades of telepathy. We hear people saying 'you have a long life' when a person you have just thought of or talked about suddenly turns up. A coincidence probably. But it could be more. It is a matter of time when science will be able to unravel the human mind. Suffice it to say that the human brain is both a transmitter and a receiver. There is the super conscious, subconscious, and the conscious. Our sages could awaken the superconscious and connect with the cosmos. This may soon be proved scientifically.

At another level, it is a truism that if you nourish positive thoughts about someone it has a way of getting transmitted to that person. It is subtle signaling at work. The same is true on the negative side. Telepathy as some of us get to experience is a random act of metaphysics, just as a ham radio homes on to a transmission as a matter of chance.

some humans die in infancy, some as young boys and girls, some in youth, some in middle age and most grow to old age when the human body is frail, wrinkled and degenerated. How do they interact when they happen to meet in the afterworlds? Do souls also age, if not how do they make out who is who?

All animals including men are born naked. As civilizations have progressed, depending upon regional factors such as culture and climate, clothing has evolved. But animals remain naked, and they look normal and even beautiful. Point, however, is up in heaven and hell, assuming these exist, how are humans attired, who provides the clothing and other with all? Who grows food, who makes it? Are there industries out there? Who runs them?

Are there colonies out there and by categories at that. As mentioned in the foregoing how do they interact? Do families join up? What is the routine? As far as the Islamic belief goes, it is endless copulation and one reckons it does not lead to reproduction, apparently. There is no mention any way as to the children that get born as a result there of. Or is it all a sham virtual experience?

In hell we are told about the eternal fire. For sinners to burn and feel the pain they must have physical bodies of flesh and bones which they have left behind on earth as decomposed material. Presumably, they get their bodies back by some magical divine process for the sadistic pleasure of God. Now consider this. The terrible fire ought to reduce the body into ash in a matter of seconds. So once that happens, one assumes that for the sinner to burn eternally in the inferno he would have to be created endlessly, till he has accounted for his sins – or is it that the body does not actually burn but is by some process is made to feel the terrible pain. It all appears so macabre and senseless. There is a belief in the Abrahamic religions that souls in heaven will get a view of hell for their enjoyment. What should one term it, perversion, or rank sadism? ("Where the worm dieth not and the fire is not quenched" – Repeated so often in the Bible).

The way the judgment day is talked about in the bible and Koran, it appears to be something that was perceived to be round the corner when the two respective books were written or so-called revealed. Apart from periodic predictions that are made by certain self-proclaimed religious big shots about an imminent apocalypse, the world has managed to survive. Now imagine the many billions of decomposed bodies turned to dust that have accumulated over millions of years or more precisely from the so-called days of Adam and Eve. Being biodegradable there can be no doubt that they have all been reabsorbed in the earth's soil system as manure etc. How and from where will these bodies rise to be taken to account as mentioned in the holy books. It is just not scientifically possible. To say that God can make anything possible is a way to avoid answering the question and is nothing but blind faith.

Look at it in another way. The human race is probably a few million years old, but it is only around 5000-8000 years BC onwards that it has continued to attain varied levels of civilized life that too unevenly. Billions of human beings have come and gone. Ninety-nine-point ninety-nine percent can be said to have led such insignificant lives, sometimes perishing in millions in natural and manmade disasters, accidents, epidemics or as cannon fodder in the wars and other forms of violence. It is as though they might as well not have been born. Would it not be a totally wasteful effort on God's part to raise these dead and to what purpose? Are the souls the way of God to perpetually keep the humans in bondage and play around with them for his self's pleasure including the sadistic one and dispense good and evil, happiness and sorrow in such an uneven and random manner. It is most unlikely and only a malevolent God would do all this.

If we look around, we will be fascinated by the regenerative process, of how the nature keeps renewing itself continuously. Every season there are fresh crops and trees bear fruits followed by harvesting, the flowers that had blown with all the glory forever die and trees shed their leaves. And so, the cycle goes on. We have seen how for instance the wheat output has grown exponentially and how from a mere 1.7 billion in 1900 AD the human population has risen to nearly 8 billion. Our animal, poultry and fish farms etc. have become like mass producing factories with least concern for animal rights. Nearly a billion plus creatures are slaughtered daily in manners most cruel for satisfying hunger, gluttony and for many their gourmet pleasure.

Animals too have feelings and they too experience pleasure and pain, happiness and sadness. Try looking into an animal's eyes, you will behold deep love, happiness, and even anger and fear in varying situations. They too have cognition and intelligence and can express their feelings. So why do the Abrahamic religions deny them their souls at par with humans? They are supposed to have material souls only, so that we can eat them without feeling unduly guilty. Though lately with a Papal decree the pets have been made an exception and are now considered to have spiritual souls like humans.

Life subsists on life. The carnivora are only performing their function because that is how nature made them. Even plants have life and have feeling. It is indeed nature's way of continuously manifesting itself both as killer and the killed, the consumer and the consumed. Vegetarianism is all about sensitivity and concern for animal life and makes sense if we want to save the environment.

A state of nonexistence is the ultimate belief in Buddhism. In Buddhist thought, rebirth does not involve any soul because of its doctrine of anatta which rejects the concept of permanent self or an unchanging, eternal soul (the Hindu belief system). According to Buddhism there is ultimately no such thing as a self in any being.

Some Buddhist traditions insist that no self-doctrine means that there is no enduring self but there is avacya (a non-self that cannot be defined) which migrates from one life to another. There are others who believe that a person's consciousness exists as a spectrum resulting in rebirth and redeath and rebecoming.

I think Richard Dawkins has the most logical answer when he says that we shall be like what we were before being born. That ought to settle matters considerably. But it is easier said than done. For the vast majority mind remains more than the mere matter of the brain, an invisible force that animates us. The Soul. The Atma.

RELIGION

Religion in its most basic form is believed to have come into existence some twelve thousand years ago with the advent of Agriculture, later metamorphosing into divergent beliefs, faiths, and modes of worship and from time to time there have been so-called revealed commands by the Almighty to his favoured messengers. Prohibitions were laid downs along with promise of rewards and threat of punishment.

It is my belief that founders of all religions were great reformers possessed of brilliant minds, who could not tolerate the evil, suffering and corrupt practices in the society, but suffered from varying forms of depression, some could be said to have been manic depressive, given to psychotic episodes and hallucinations whereby they convinced themselves and their followers that they were in direct contact with God/gods or their agents. We should also not discount charlatans among them with some of them even faking their psychotic – like experiences during spiritual trances and passing them on as revelations from the almighty. We also know the tricks illusionists can conjure up which are passed on by godmen as miracles to their followers. There is also the phenomenon of covert mass hypnosis. We need to have an open mind in all this.

We have also seen that whenever an existing religion or society becomes corrupted, dissolute, or diffused, a messiah invariably emerges who manages to give a new focus of meaning and in the bargain starts a new cult or religion.

Basically, all religions get to serve the same purpose. Food, air, water, shelter, sex [procreation] and sleep are man's primary needs. But over-riding all these are the existential ones which are essential for our emotional and mental wellbeing. Some people place the recreational activities viz; sports, music, and hobbies among the basic needs but this is debatable because the emotional dividend of recreational activities is substantial. Nevertheless, religion remains the most common means by which people get to fulfil their existential needs. It provides emotional stability and security, allays our fears, and makes us believe in the supreme being to whom we can turn for succour. There is that hunger for cosmic support. Sceptics call it the God delusion but for the common man religion provides solace through belief in God, a sense of holiness and a meaning and purpose in life and the urge to do righteous deeds as ordained in our respective faiths. It provides man with joy, a deep sense of contentment and inner peace even in midst of sorrow.

But there is also the very dark side of religion. Religion has continued to divide mankind and has been the cause of terrible violence and suffering. Bertrand Russel has described religion as a disease born of fear and source of untold misery to human race and primarily a social phenomenon. Fear according to him is the basis of the whole thing. Fear is the parent of cruelty and no wonder religion and cruelty have gone hand in hand. Religion is fettering of intelligence by words uttered long ago by ignorant men.

In religion there is hostility to hard scientific evidence. Religion causes us to close our minds to every fact that does not suit its ingrained prejudices. Religion demands total submission and faith. Come to think of it, what is faith? Basically, faith consists in believing not what seems true but what seems false to our understanding. Faith consists in believing things because they are impossible.

"Tell a devout Christian that Frozen Yogurt can make a man invisible", so writes Sam Harris, "and he is likely to require as much evidence as anyone else and persuaded only to the extent that you can provide it. Tell him that the book he keeps by his bed side was written by an invisible deity, who will punish him with fire for eternity if he fails to accept its very incredible claims, he seems to require no evidence whatsoever".

Judaism, Christianity, and Islam are religions of the same book, and yet throughout history have been consistently at each other's throats though Islam's claim on the Old Testament appears unconvincing, considering that the Arabs prior to the birth of Islam were hugely polytheistic and the veil around the Kaaba is mystifying to say the least. Nevertheless, all three religions believe in Satan or Lucifer, angels, saints, and various demonical characters. So, if their God could create or cohabit with all these entities, what prevents him from creating lesser gods to whom he could conveniently delegate power and responsibility which would all be for the good. Surely God who is supreme beyond imagination cannot be so jealous, vindictive, vengeful, insecure, and possessive as he is made out to be.

Having said the above it is difficult to refute the power of prayer, granted most prayers may go unanswered but there are cases where the outcome is quite often spectacular. The phenomenon of mind over body is a fact of life. That faith can literally move mountains cannot be denied. There can be no doubt that all this is based upon some scientific law whereby positive energy so released makes things happen. Opposite is also true where negative thinking makes what is most feared to happen. Science is yet discover all the secrets of human mind and harness its immense power and possibilities.

HINDUISM

Hinduism is vast, most complex, unorganized, immersed in great deal of symbolism, rituals, and metaphysical thoughts. It is steeped in idol worship, but its essence is its deep spiritualism which can be both sublime and subtle. Hindu devotional music, the various ragas, hymns and bhajans are soul lifting. Hindus love to celebrate their gods and their festivals are colourful and even chaotic. To a casual observer Hinduism may appear as paganism but this is only the superficial part, as the Hindu belief systems are derived from a pantheon of gods as given in their holy texts; Vedas, Upanishads, Puranas, the two epics Ramayana and Mahabharat and most revered of all is the Bhagvad Gita. There are also esoteric and even bizarre cults verging on the occult and the macabre. Their practitioners are the Hindu odd balls, and they too have their followers.

The present somewhat sullied by times Hinduism has its roots in a utopian past, with hardly a parallel in the history of mankind. After the golden period of the Gupta dynasty, there was a long civilizational plateau, nearly five centuries of peace and prosperity when India was a land of milk and honey where man lived in harmony with nature. The Adivasis inhabiting the jungles and forests enjoyed a unique kind of autonomy. The wild animals were protected by religious laws.

Manu's laws were in force. Nearly a thousand castes and subcastes coexisted and diligently followed their specified tasks and professions. Wars between various Hindu kingdoms (Palas, Pratihars and Chandels) were converted into sportive events with chivalry and valour as their hallmarks. This was a period of great intellectual activity when literature and fine arts flourished. The Puranas were rewritten and revised. There were treatises galore on religion, philosophy, Ayurveda, mathematics, and astronomy. With centuries of uninterrupted peace, the Hindu society turned soft. It became the time for romance and abandonment to sex and pleasure. Prolonged peace brought with it a false sense of security and gradually degeneration and decay set in, with it, permissiveness, and promiscuity. Hindu became indolent and a debauch as he began to worship the erotica. Fornication, adultery, orgies and even perversion became part of public life through the medium of literature and sculpture, the finest examples being Khajuraho temples and Vatsyan's Kamasutra. The Hindu was busy having a good time till Islam came and spoilt the party. Caught unaware, in warfare he was in most cases no match to the Islamic invaders, who were hardier and superior in tactics, surprise, deception, maneuver and fire power. Not that there was dearth of valour, it was the herbivorous bull fighting a hungry and ferocious carnivorous animal. There were many acts of bravery, but these were self-destructive in nature.

The Hindu was reduced to being a subject and vanquished race, but inherent strength of Hindu culture and ethos began to gradually reassert itself. The Hindus successfully resisted conversion to Islam in any significant numbers barring the lower castes who were attracted by the egalitarianism of Islam. The Hindus absorptive ways led to the process of assimilation. They continued to vastly outnumber the Muslims in the subcontinent and with the passage of time ended up being generally better off in most fields. It was the Hindu blood in Mohammed Iqbal that made him pen these lines about the Hindu enigma: -

"Yunan-o-Misr-o- Roma Sab Mit Gaye Jahan Se, Ab Tak Magar Hai Baki Naam-o-Nishan Hamara, Kuchh Baat Hai Ke Hasti Mit'ti Nahin Hamari, Sadiyon Raha Hai Dushman Daur-e-Zaman Hamara"

While most Hindu heritage in the shape of temples and seats of learning in the northern parts of India came to be destroyed, South India largely escaped the Muslim onslaught and is in fact today the home of the purer form of Hinduism with marvelous temples, devotional music, and classical dance disciplines. Various kingdoms of South India namely Cholas, Pandyas and Pallavas flourished and spread across the Bay of Bengal to Myanmar, Thailand, Cambodia, Laos, Vietnam, and Indonesia. For five centuries the powerful Vijaynagar Empire thwarted southward invasion by the Muslim invaders. In the east the Ahom kingdom of Assam remained unvanquished till the annexation by the British in the nineteenth century.

But the fact is that for four hundred years most of India was under the Muslim rule followed by a hundred to two hundred years under the British and all this was to deal a debilitating blow to the psyche of the shehri (urban) Hindu and produced a narrative that is largely derogatory and earnt the Hindus all kinds of pejoratives like effete, servile, weird, and other unmentionable slights. Impressions die hard and turn into strong beliefs and prejudices. Truth is the casualty. The bulk of India's population lives in the villages comprising of simple and courageous peasantry, who have continuously provided India with the finest soldiers in the world; Rajputs, Dogras, Jats, Gujjars, Ahirs, Marathas, Garhwalis, Kumaonis, Malayali Nairs, Coorgs, Tamil and Telugu. There are also the Gurkhas who are Hindus and Sikhs who descended from the Hindus. During the British Raj, the Muslims formed thirty percent of the British Indian Army. Interestingly if you go through the list of the gallantry awards during the two world wars, you will find that nearly ninety percent of these were won by the non-Muslim soldiers.

It is well known that majority of Hindus are vegetarians, and they hold cows as sacred. Coming to the negatives most Hindus are superstitious and ardent believers in horoscope and astrology. Guided by auspicious and inauspicious moments, they invoke their many gods for worldly gains, though theirs may not be the only community that indulges in this practice. They mostly follow some godman or guru, many of whom are outright fakes who exploit their blind followers. The Hindu's chief concern is for self and his family and a better karma. Untouchability now officially banned is an evil that has yet to be fully eradicated and brings the Hindus a bad name. The Hindu society has been continuously undergoing reforms over the last two hundred years from the banning of the practice of sati, to ending polygamy and child marriage, empowerment of women, and ending the plight of the widows. It remains a work in progress in our form of democracy.

There are also many virtues in Hinduism. There is great tolerance and religious freedom enjoyed equally even by atheists. India has throughout its history provided refuge to persecuted minorities from other countries like Jews, Parsees and more recently the Tibetan Buddhists and the Dalai Lama much to the chagrin and consternation of Communist China.

BUDDHISM

Buddhism began in India in the Fifth; Sixth centuries BCE as a Sramana tradition (earliest anti-Brahmanical movement). Theory or concept of karma is the core belief in Buddhism. Karma is action/work and includes the thought process. Good and bad Karma accumulates even if there is no physical action. Having ill or good thoughts creates karmic seeds. Action of body, speech or mind all lead to good and bad karma. It operates like the laws of physics, without external intervention, on all beings and covers all six realms of existence as understood in Buddhism. The central theme is attainment of merit, more the better for overcoming dukkha, for attaining noble rebirth and for the flawless the state of nonexistence or Nirvana. There is also the method where merit can be transferred to near and dear one. The rebirth depends on the merit or demerit gained by one's karma, as well as that get accrued on one's behalf by a family member.

There are six realms into which rebirth can occur of which three are good and the other three evil. The three good realms are heavenly, demi-god and human. The evil ones are animals, hungry ghosts and hellish. Samsara ends if a person attains Nirvana, which happens by blowing out of all desires and gaining the true insight into the impermanence and non-self-reality.

Dharma in Buddhism encompasses virtues such as wisdom, kindness, patience, generosity, and compassion. There are five moral percepts which prohibit killing living things, taking what is not given, sexual misconduct, lying and using drugs or alcohol.

The two most defining features of Buddhism are the Four Noble Truths and the Eightfold Path and form the essence of this unique religion.

The Four Noble Truths which are essential to understanding Buddhism are: -

1. Suffering (dukkha) caused by longing and desire.

2. Ignorance of reality's true nature.

3. Impermanence (anicca)

4. Non-existence of the self

Dukkha arises when we crave and cling to desires. Clinging and craving for sense pleasures produces karma, which ties us to samsara and thereby to death and rebirth. Dukkha ceases when craving and attachment cease. This means no more karma is being produced and thereby rebirth ends and a state of non-existence or nirvana ensues.

Once realization of the Four Noble Truths has been achieved the true Buddhist has to follow the 'Eightfold Path': -

1. Right Understanding

2. Right Thought

3. Right speech

4. Right Action

5. Right livelihood

6. Right effort

7. Right mindfulness

8. Right concentration.

In theory Buddhism is the most rational religion in the world and it is all about good conduct and spiritualism. Life is well ordered and disciplined and there is reverence and serenity, but we are dealing with human nature which has its many failings. It is therefore only natural that Buddhism too would be affected by various ills and compromises. There are known cases of corruption, other malpractices, and sexual abuse.

One of its basic beliefs of Buddhism is non-violence and not killing living things and yet we see that most

Buddhists are meat eaters and especially in China and other east Asian countries they eat literally anything that moves from snails to snakes, bats, cockroaches, and all kinds of insects. They are especially fond of pork. There is undoubtedly a well-reasoned explanation for this phenomenon, the most likely being that it was just not possible for these societies to change age old eating habits caused by environmental compulsions. But there has been large scale violence against fellow humans too. The Sinhalese Army, which is chiefly Buddhist, is guilty of massacring the Tamilians. There have been large scale killings in Cambodia and Myanmar. The Japanese during the Second World War were totally ruthless.

Is the crime rate less among the Buddhists? Given the tenets of Buddhism and the fact most Buddhists follow their religion quite diligently and it indeed appears to be so when one looks at the life in Bhutan, Ladakh, Lahaul and Spiti, Sikkim and Arunachal Pradesh. It would be reasonable to assume that situation would be about the same in the other Buddhist countries. One thing is for certain they outscore the Hindus, Muslims and even Christians when it comes to happiness index. In the final analysis it can be said that most Buddhists have pursued and continue to pursue rituals and practices seeking better rebirth not nirvana. There is much ado around the search of reincarnate Lamas.

CHRISTIANITY

The First Word comprising of Europe, North America, Australia, and New Zealand is all Christian. It is rich, modern, prosperous, emancipated and life generally is good. But it is not overtly religious except for some of the southern states of the USA. There is racism but that is a different matter. Its foundation are the Greek and Roman civilizations. It has witnessed renaissance, scientific, and industrial revolutions, and two centuries of enlightenment and free thought. Atheism is gradually on the rise. The Christian Whites have ruled the world during the last four centuries. They have made stupendous inventions, discoveries in science and technology for which lot of credit should go the White Jews. The spirit of discovery, sports and of adventure covering terrestrial, aero and aqua mediums and recreational activities are mostly of western origin and now practiced all over the world. Christianity as it is practiced today is much refined. There is great dignity and solemnity. But it has not always been like this. Christianity has gone through a very dark and gruesome stage. Militant Islam and terror as we see today would pale in comparison with the cruelties that the Christians inflicted on themselves and the world and even now there are enough skeletons that routinely keep tumbling out of both the Catholic and

Protestants unholy cupboards. Christian history is full of tales of inquisition with untold torture, where a few hundred thousand (may be many more) heretics and women (charged as witches) were beheaded and burnt on the stakes. There was every kind of cruelty practiced upon all sorts of people in the name of religion.

Jesus Christ believed in hell. This profoundly humane person believed in eternal punishment and there seems to be hint of a certain pleasure in his description of the scene in hell – the wailing and gnashing of teeth of the sinners. He could get very irritated with people who disagreed with his teachings or did not like his preaching. He would curse them, call them serpents and vipers fit for damnation and hell.

There is also the curious story where Christ cursed the fig tree for none of its fault because it could not produce the out of season fruit to quench his pressing hunger and as a result had to simply wither away.

Christ had said "Resist not evil but whosoever shall smite thee on thy right cheek, turn to him the other also". But this is not the principle the Christians ever practiced. On the contrary they colonized whole continents and exterminated the indigenous population of aborigines in Americas, Australia, New Zealand, and parts of Africa. European history itself is full of continuous warfare and bloodshed right till the Second World War.

Christian argument that suffering in the world is a purification of sin and therefore a good thing smacks of cruelty and insensitivity. What sins could children stricken with cancer and other terrible ailments and deformities have committed for their terrible suffering. We have often seen it is the good people who have committed no sins who mostly suffer unless we believe that they are carrying the cross for the sins of others or believe in the theory of Karma of the Hindus.

There are the Christian missionaries active among the poor of the world and doing their bit for alleviating poverty and suffering and running orphanages, but the driving force is proselytization. In India for over a century now they have been poaching on the periphery of Hinduism and have been quite successful, especially in India's northeast and it has not been a bad thing though. It has given these people a dignified way of life. Buddhism may have been a better alternative.

ISLAM

There is a great vitality inherent in the uncomplicated teachings of Islam and a unique spirit of egalitarianism that has fascinated and attracted millions of followers over the centuries. There is the magic of Sufism. It was a great reformatory movement of its times which continued to evolve and witnessed its golden age from the days of Harun ul Rashid in the eighth to the mid-thirteenth century with Baghdad as its capital. It was one of the greatest periods of human flourishment in knowledge and progress till the horrific sack of Baghdad by the Mongols under Hulagu Khan in 1258. It is a different matter that the Mongols themselves were to soon thereafter convert to Islam and Islam continued to expand to whole of Central and South Asia and North Africa and parts of Europe, but things would never be the same.

There is the other side too where the Islamic invaders caused much destruction and bloodshed, particularly in India where they destroyed thousands of Hindu and Buddhist temples and places of learning like Taxila and Nalanda and there are accounts of untold rape and genocide. The last three centuries in the history of Islam have been those of regression, fratricide internecine conflicts.

Those who think that Islam is all about voluptuousness and sensuality need to seriously rethink. During the holy month of Ramzan, the faithful do not drink [not even a drop of water] or eat from four in the morning till eight at night, given that Ramzan mostly falls during the summer. It requires extreme self-discipline and will power. A Muslim is forbidden to play any game of chance under pain of damnation and consumption of alcohol is similarly forbidden and so is the practice of usury and he must set aside a part of his earnings for charity called Zaqat.

Driving motivation of Islam is also no doubt sexual empowerment of man. He has complete control over his women who like in orthodox Christianity are considered sex objects, inspirers of lust and temptation. They are his property. He can have four legitimate wives and as many mistresses/concubines that he can afford. He can divorce and remarry. He has divine sanction to have sex slaves as part of war bounty.

When we say he owns his women, their bodies and hence they must remain in purdah to avoid the lustful glance of other men. For many Muslim women it also gives a sense of security. Need of rape of own women is not necessary because he can have them whenever he feels like, but rape of non-Muslims is a bonus and has divine sanction. There are ills like triple talaq, nikah halala and mutation of female genitals which are highly condemnable.

Though much is made of virgins it must be conceded that in Islam divorce, remarriage including by the widows is the norm. Compare this with Hinduism; the extremely sad lives the widows led, and many continue to lead, obsession with chastity and female feticide. Marriage in Islam is a contract which is a very sensible thing and no wonder in all other religions despite pious vows divorce is now quite the normal thing.

There is also great effrontery about Islam. It is not only contemptuous of other faiths, but it won't also leave them alone and the extreme elements routinely abuse and curse the infidels and call for their liquidation through conversion, ethnic cleansing or outright killing. This religion of peace has a creed of intolerance, violence and Jihad running parallel to it. All contradictions are taken care of and justified; one must simply look for the relevant surahs of their holy book.

Will there be a time when Muslims will start questioning the life of Mohammed in the manner the Christians have gone into the life of Jesus Christ?

EXISTENTIALISM IN ISLAM

Mohammad Ibrahim Zauq

Mohammad Ibrahim Zauq was a religious and literary scholar and the poet laurate of the Mughal Court in Delhi (mid-19th Century) in the time of Bahadur Shah Zafar, the last of the Moghul emperors. My father who was well versed in Persian and Urdu used to sometimes recite the under given poem of Zauq, that so aptly describes the enigma that is life.

Layi hayaat aye qaza le chali chale

Na apni khushi aye na apni khushi chale

Behtar to yahi hai na duniya se dil lage

Par kya karen kam na bedillagi chale

Ho umr-e-khizr to kahenge bevaqt-e marg

ham kya rahe yahan abhi aye abhi chale

Duniya ne kis ka rahe fana mein diya hai saath

Tum bhi chale chalo yun hi jab tak chale chale

Nazar na ho khirad pe jo hona hai wahi to

Danish teri na kuchh meri danish vari chale

Kam honge is bisat pe hum jaise budqimar

Jo chaal hum chale who nihayat buri chale

Jate hava-e shauq mein hain is chaman se Zauq

Apni bala se baad-saba jahan kahin chale

[Life brought me here and death shall take me away. No one sought my permission for sending me here nor will my accord be sought for my departure. Would it therefore not be better if I could but stay away from getting involved in this worldly life but how can I enjoy my work without getting emotionally involved in it. Even if my life's span is long, having begun my life the feeling that it is already time to leave is never far away. And when has anyone in this world ever accompanied any other on our respective journeys to annihilation, it is our lot to also to continue walking alone on the path as long as the path goes. Neither will all our wisdom nor all our intelligence change anything or make any difference. Indeed, this game of chess that is life, we are often so bad at playing it, whatever move we make, it turns out to be a badly played one. And finally, bidding farewell, I leave this garden amid inner winds of joy, why should I care if the pleasant morning breeze is blowing elsewhere.]

Omar Khayam

Omar Khayyam was a Twelfth century Persian mathematician, philosopher and a Sufi poet influenced by Zoroastrianism, the religion of Persia before the onset of Islam in that country. It is not certain how much of his rubaiyats as translated by Edward Fitzgerald an Englishman in 1859 are authentically his or have been suitably modified by Fitzgerald but nonetheless reveal a rare blend of skepticism and existentialism. I have found it worth the while to share ten of them for their subtlety and depth.

1

And, as the cock crew, those who stood before

The Tavern shouted – "Open then the door!

You know how little we have to stay

And once departed, may return no more."

2

Come, fill the cup, and in the Fire of Spring

The Winter Garment of Repentance fling:

The Bird of Time has but a little way

To fly – and Lo! The bird is on the wing.

3

Ah, my beloved, fill the cup that clears

To-day of past Regrets and future Fears

To-morrow – Why, To-morrow I may be

Myself with Yesterday's seven thousand years

4

Ah, make the most of what we yet may spend,

Before we too into the Dust descend.

Dust into Dust, and under Dust, to lie,

Sans Wine, sans Song, sans Singer, and – sans End

5

Alike for those who for Today prepare,

And those that after some Tomorrow stare,

A Muezzin from the tower of Darkness cries,

"Fools your Reward is neither Here nor There.

6

There was a Door to which I found no Key.

There was the Veil past which I could not see.

Some little talk awhile of Me and Thee

There was – and then no more of Thee and Me.

7

Oh, threats of Hell and Hopes of Paradise!

One thing is certain – This Life flies:

One thing is certain, and the rest is lies.

The Flower that once is blown forever dies

8

The Moving Finger writes; and, having writ,

Moves on, nor all your Piety nor Wit.

Shall lure it back to cancel half a line,

Nor all your tears wash out a Word of it.

9

And that inverted Bowl we call the Sky,

Where under crawling coop'd we live and die,

Lift not your hands to it for help - for it

As impotently rolls as you or I.

10

Said one among them – "Surely not in vain,

My Substance from the common Earth was taken.

That who subtly wrought me into shape.

Should stamp me back to shapeless Earth again?

SIKHISM

Sikhism began as a sect of Hinduism and was started by Guru Nanak, the noblest of souls, a later-day Buddha, who too wandered far and wide in search of truth and finally declared that karam yoga – an honest householder's life spent in worship of one supreme God was the true path in life. He was a great reformer and did away with idol worship and many a superstition that the subject and passive Hindu society under the Muslim rule that he was born into, followed.

Sikhism is to my knowledge the only religion in the world that is devoid of all negativities, all kinds of fears and concepts like auspicious and inauspicious moments. The three laudable tenets of Sikhism; remembering God constantly, earning an honest livelihood and sharing one's earnings with the needy are its defining features. One is unlikely to come across a beggar who is Sikh. Sikhism is Sanatam Dharma in its most sublime and simple form despite the radicals, who beginning with the Tat Khalsa in 1920s, with a kind of Oedipus complex, have been resorting to distortions to distance Sikhism from its Hindu roots. They are living in denial and in the bargain are doing a great disservice to their great religion. They have been spending lot of energy and effort to prove that Sikhism is not Hinduism, which of course it is not, just as Protestants are not the same as Catholics. Sikhs have their distinct identity, their sacred text, a proud history replete with sacrifices of the extreme kind by three of their Gurus and many other martyrs. The fact is that Indic mythology permeates the Sikh Sacred Canon, the Adi Granth and especially the Dasham Granth and most of the composition is in Brijbhasha. Gurmukhi is a hybrid of Devanagiri and landa (Brahmi derived mercantile script). It has been mentioned a couple of times in the sacred text that there is no Hindu and no Musalman and that all humans are one and the same and a few other similar invocations. This is very much in line with the age-old Sanatam Dharma philosophy, the concept of 'Vasudeva Kutumbkam' – The world is one. The point is as to how the Muslims look at it for whom the only God is Allah. The Sikh concept of one supreme God is in line with Nirguna and in that sense monotheistic.

All Sikh Gurus were proud Khatris, and all married with in the caste, though not all succession was always smooth. Bedis and Sodhis hold a special place among the Sikhs. They obviously practiced the caste system. What they propounded was equality and a discrimination and prejudice free society.

It would be worth checking the number of Muslims who converted to Sikhism. While it may not be zero, certainly the numbers are insignificant. It was Muslim rule in Punjab when Sikhism was born. While there appears to have been a fair amount of tolerance and co-existence among the Muslims and Hindus till the time of Jehangir, the Mullahs and the then administration would never have permitted Muslim conversion to Sikhism. The very content of the Granth Sahib with repeated invocation and even celebration of the Hindu gods, the inclusion of dohas of Baba Farid, the Muslim Sufi, notwithstanding, is an anathema to the Muslim psyche. The Sikhs faced absolutely no persecution till the time of the first four Gurus as Sikhism was considered like any other Hindu sect. It was under the fifth Guru, Guru Arjun Dev when Sikhism started to become a socio moral force to reckon with and a visible threat that the persecution started, and the Guru was tortured and martyred.

Mardana's close relations with Guru Nanak are much spoken about, yet he remained a Muslims as also his descendants and the present generation lives on in Pakistan as devout Muslims and keeps up with the Marasi community's tradition as musicians. On the other hand, Guru Nanak is known to have forcefully exhorted Lehna, who later became Guru Angad, to give up Devi worship and instead become his follower.

Guru Shishya has been centuries old tradition in India from ancient times. Sikhism as the name suggests was very much that. Among the Hindus it was and remains this way when they follow different gurus and godmen and yet retain their Hindu faith. So certainly, till very recently when Hindus in large numbers adopted Sikhism, they never consciously broke away more so socially from their parent faith.

POETIC LICENSE

This final chapter consists of a set of poems written by the author, summarising his views on God and Religion have an element of irreverence and satire and is meant to be taken in that spirit.

1

Lord God I often think of you.

I was weak I prayed a lot.

I am still weak I sometimes do.

Who are you?

Do you also have your God as helpless as you?

Holy Brahmin and other bigoted lot

I seek not I seek you.

You are elusive. Why?

Tell me God

Do animals have their God?

I mean you.

Their straightforward ways

Their honesty and lack of deceit

Man was OK.

When he lived with them

There was the unwritten law of the jungle.

Till he broke it and made his own

And created you.

And the license to first devour the animals.

And then the Earth

As he now heads to the stars.

3

God! Who are you?

Over a drink I ask

False boldness in pursuit of truth

Where are you when terrible things happen?

Are you a Raja or a Faqir?

Your million temples million mosques and Christ's holy
churches

This narrow-minded stuff you allow it all.

Did man create you in selfish mood?

One man's business made everyone else's.

These possessed revolutionaries these zealous
reformers.

causing catastrophes and mighty upheavals

They cheat mankind and drive it to eternal slavery.

They make you personal which you are not.

They tell there is one God, but they lie.

There are many Gods.

Hindu, Muslim, Christian and how many others?

These pretenders, these great prophets

They hallucinate and fox the world for capturing power.

These social outcastes, they seek revenge.

They enslave mankind causing mighty fear.

They begin covertly.

These great reformers

In the name of you they create religions

And then they die but the mischief is done

Forever dividing mankind

Man against man the game goes on.

4

There is the Hindu God

Nirguna the unmanifested

And many ages of Brahma

The Trinity and their Avatars

And then the manifested chaos
A thousand gods their many wives

Each a goddess
Since they mate, they are happy.
So also, the Hindus
On prorata basis, it depends on your caste.
The learned Brahmin, his soft body
Ghee, aarti and incense
Worshipping Dravidian gods of Mohenjo-Daro times
A crazy pantheon of grotesque shapes and Pagan rites
Of burning ghats, the gates of fire
Bhootnath overseeing it all.
A philosophy corrupted by time.
Licensed obscenities and fatalistic minds
The auspicious and not so moments
Superstitions of the absurd kind
Psychedelic worship, its sensuous derivations
Bliss peace and meditation
Themes of karma when gods are bribed.
For small and big prize
Renunciation; the abjuring by the worldly wise
Festivals of Holi, Dussehra and Diwali
And many other days and nights
Colour, music, frolic, solemnity, and lights

Kumbh Melas when millions assemble.

Thousand sects in warlike camps

It is devotion in their eyes.

Himalaya of the eternal snows – abode of gods

Ancient uncomplicated shrines

Breathtaking scenery amidst awe inspiring heights

Cold and with fresh air in his lungs

Hindu's search for peace seems so real.

Dawn and dusk by the Ganga

Washing sins off mankind

evening Aarti, the rising crescendo

Conches, bells and sound of masses

in ecstatic, pious and chanting delight

Cult of abstract peace and terrible violence

Animal and even human sacrifice

Enlightened and decayed minds

Thieves, brigands, thugs and prostitutes

all have their presiding deities.

Vedas, Upanishads, Bhagavad Gita and Kamasutra

Arya Samajis, their fundamentalism set in ancient
times.

It is utter confusion if you pause to think.

Sublime to the ridiculous It is a great religion,

nay a way of life sans pretensions

You need never practice what is preached.

It is the flower Children's' delight.

On which the Brahmins, the Tantric

Godmen and charlatans thrive.

Friends, when I was a child.

A certain day every year grandfather and all family

worshipped the clan's Sati at her shrine.

Somehow, I always thought she was a beautiful woman.

It was a silent secret love.

but a thousand years divided us.

5

Have visited many a Buddhist shrine.

Catholic ambience and sweep of true peace.

Mournful music issuing within dark frescoed walls.

Silent conjuring and chanting with cymbal.

Lest demons be awake

As they sleep underground, in crevices deep.

Lest they rove in fog and on mountain tops

Causing death and spirits to Devil sold

Chhang! Man, buttered tea and feasts.

Soiled pages of a thousand jatakas

Om Mani Padme Hum, mani walls on road and by
riverside

Chortens and stupas with holy relics in search of peace

Prayer wheels by hand and by water run.

The wheels of Karma

Prayer streamers fluttering in high wind.

Seeking absolution or Nirvana

The lama with his many wives and chelas

guarantees all this.

if you leave your soul with him

ceremonies, he will perform.

Birth, marriage and death

Year of the rabbit or the lion

He will see to it all.

Go western but burn your lamps.

Not to forget excess of chhang and rakshi

Lama will see to it all.

Your cycles of births and your dead body's direction
from the house

And Buddha since he had no grave, cannot stir.

But quizzes over his meaningful penance

Under the ancient banyan tree

6

I thought I was a Christian at heart.

I was confusing the Western civilization with the
Christian religion.

Deep down it's the same bigotry.

Like others its belief is in a personalized God

Who is both kind and cruel?

Retribution and luridly described scenes of hell

Thousands of conscious years of mankind

And God's affairs with Lucifer still not resolved.

It's unfair to blame the ever erring mankind

Arms of peace supplied by the Christian white.

Would they be prosperous otherwise?

The zealous missionary, his concern for human
suffering not denied.

his condescending ways and righteousness so affected.

These colonisers exact a subtle price.

multiplying Christ's flock in distant lands

with deceit and inducements of better life

The heathens have little choice.

Proclaiming damnation for trivial sins when greater
evils go unheeded by

The padres, bishops and nuns alike

Indulging in child abuse and leading perverted lives

And rarely confessing their sexual crimes

The Papal mystique and blessed mankind

Catholics and protestants and their many churches

The Mass and the Service, Baptism, Marriage and Last
Rites

The serene cemeteries and uncanny epitaphs

The child laying a rose by the graveside.

There is human dignity when you hold your head high.

Somehow it just ends there.

And then the awry right who spoil everything

What peace there would be on this earth

If they just practiced it right

There is a selfishness about them.

Manifested in ways so unkind.

The Christians have usurped a mighty civilization.

By their outward adventurous ways

The white race has ruled and will rule for its span of
time.

It is the wheel and turn of time.

That moves and moves and then the demise.

7

Alaf Lam Mim

Allah be praised.

For all his mercies

He is all forgiving.

And compassionate

Glory to him

And the Prophet

In the name of God

Where does the mischief start?

It doesn't seem to end anyway.

Believer and infidel alike

Tread you carefully.

Beware thou of holy chastisement.

That lies ahead, the hell's eternal fire.

Believe you me it's all very frightening!

Await the Doomsday.

When souls rise

Should you behave?

There is much you can gain.

Gardens beneath which rivers flow

Pleasures of purified Houries

Does that imply earthly women be impure?

A man's possession for his pleasure with laid down
rules.

Poor thing she must learn to bear it.

Or fight for her rights

Just two alternatives

Believe or be condemned.

Bliss or damnation

And enslaved mankind

Unable to question or revise.

The dictates of a brilliant man

Helplessly follows the reforms.

Meant for premedieval times.

Dare they question the rationale.

How come from the days of Old Testament?

So many thousands of years God has had enough time.

To settle his score with the Devil and all his evil

Poor the man is left with little choice.

God won't vanquish Satan.

I wonder what the game is all about

Why must the Shias and Sunnis fight

Why must God fight his private wars?

Through this crazy mankind

For the sake of a promised land

Surely, if it isn't here.

It is nowhere.

8

The Sikhs say they are different.

Quam and a Religion

Why not?

They have a right like all others.

Tough, heroic, and warm hearted

Clean, forthcoming, and spontaneous

Turbulent, and tremendous enterprise

A profound history of martyrdom and great sacrifice

And that sense of humour

Jat, Ramdassia, Majhbi, Ramgarhia

And the Bhapa or the Khatri

And Karha Prasad

Gurudwara, ardaas and councils of war

Hymns and the soothing sabad kirtan

Worshipping Granth Sahib

As most Hindus the idols do

Fighting their legacy and their Hindu roots

Nanak thought he was building a bridge.

Or was he fighting his own conscience?

Of being born among subject passive Hindus

under the Muslim rule

Friends don't get me wrong.

It's only a theory of mine

The later day Buddha In search of God and truth

Forsook renunciation and idol worship.

Through good karma he Nirvana sought

But what of his bridge, someone ought to know

Sikhism once the most positive of religions

Now has its share of bigotry and fanaticism.

9

Friends I have no illusions.

No utopian ideas

No alternatives

Worship what you will

It keeps the shrinks at bay.

We all must die one day.

Religion is the great opium.

That drugs the people.

Especially the poor

Power flows through the poor

Over a few centuries and sometime a millennium

A brilliant mind encashes this great power

It includes communism.

When they lynch kill and plunder

Murderous orgies let loose.

By maniacs and saints

Malicious manipulators

Causing death of countless innocents

Live and let live.

Only great rulers make that happen.

When they bring about equality and justice

Tolerance and quality of life

Education of the higher kind

Let us hope for the best.

That one fine day

There will be peace on this earth.

And when that happens

There will be a true civilization.

That would have overcome tyranny of fear.

BIBLIOGRAPHY

1. Portable Voltaire – Editor Ben Ray Redman – Penguin Books 1950

2. Why I am not a Christian – Bertrand Russel – Simon and Schuster 1950

3. Rubaiyat of Omar Khayyam (Rendered into English by E Fitzgerald) Collins 1954

4. God Delusion – Richard Dawkins – Society for Promotion of Christian Knowledge – 20007

5. The End of Faith – Sam Harris -WW Norton 2004

6. God is not Great – Christopher Hitchens – Hachette Book Group 2007

7. The Four Horsemen – Penguin Random House UK – 2019

8. The Bhagavadgita – S Radhakrishnan – Harper Collins 2010

9. Voice of Reason – Onkar Goraya – Notion Press 2021

10. Internet - Wikipedia

OTHER BOOKS BY THE AUTHOR

1. The Call of Everest

2. A Mountain of Happiness

3. When Generals Failed (The Chinese Invasion 1962)

4. Security Peace and Honour

5. Pakistan our Difficult Neighbour and Allied Issues

6. Pakistan our Difficult Neighbour and India's Islamic Dimensions

7. Themes of Glory (Indian Artillery in War)

Brigadier Darshan Khullar was born in Bassi Pathanan, Punjab in 1941 and educated at Rashtriya Indian Military College (formerly The Prince of Wales Royal Indian Military College), Dehradun. A soldier mountaineer and author, he has led nine successful expeditions to Himalaya peaks, the most notable being the Indian Everest Expedition in 1984 when the First Indian woman (Bachendri Pal) reached the summit.

He is the recipient of Padma Shri and Arjuna Awards and Ati Vishist Sewa Medal (AVSM). He has authored several books on mountaineering, political science, and military history.